Wicked Jokes

to make you giggle!

Chuckle Hee Ha Ha Ha Chortle

Tee Hee Ha Giggle Hee Hee Titter
Ha Hee

Tee
Hee

Ha

Ha

Hee

Ha

Tee

Hee

Hee

Ha

Ha

Ha

Tee
Hee

Ha

Ha

Hee

Ha

Tee

Hee

Hee

Ha

Ha

Ha

This book belongs to:

Hee Hee Tee Chortle Ha Ha Ha
Ha Hee Ha Ha Ha Tee Hee
Chuckle Ha Ha Hee Hee Chortle

Wicked Jokes

to make you giggle!

Marks and Spencer p.l.c.
PO Box 3339, Chester CH99 9QS
www.marksandspencer.com

Copyright © Exclusive Editions 2004

This book was created by Magpie Books,
an imprint of Constable & Robinson Ltd

Inside illustrations
courtesy of Mike Phillips

A copy of the British Library
Cataloguing-in-Publication Data is
available from the British Library

Printed in China

ISBN 1-84461-189-2

Contents:

Happy Howlers

What language do they
speak in Cuba?
Cubic.

Why couldn't the wigwam
and tepee get to sleep?
Because they were
two tents.

What instrument did they
play in the Middle Ages?
The Anglo-saxophone.

What do you get if you
cross a skeleton, a feather
and a joke book?
Rib ticklers.

What's the best way
to make a coat last?
Make the trousers first.

Why did the seaweed blush?
Because it saw the
ship's bottom.

What is a bunsen
burner used for?
Burning bunsens.

What do you get if you
cross a skeleton with
a tumble drier?
Bone-dry clothes.

When is a grown man
still a child?
When he's a miner.

What's the difference
between a cat and a comma?
One has claws at the end of
her paws and the other has a
pause at the end of a clause.

What do you get if you
wash your greenhouse?
Broken glass in the
washing machine.

How do you strain
vegetables?
Make them do a hundred
press-ups and a
ten-mile run.

How do you get a baby
astronaut to sleep?
Rock it.

Why was the man with
£1999.99 in his hands unwell?
He wasn't feeling
too grand.

What's a spaceman's
favourite meal?
Launch.

What do people do in
clock factories?
They make faces all day.

What do computer experts
do at weekends?
Go for a disk drive.

How do you make
hot cross buns?
Lock buns in a room and
turn the heating up high.

What did the hungry
alien say when he
landed on Earth?
"Take me to your larder!"

How do you make
a Swiss roll?
Push him off a mountain.

What do a footballer and a
magician have in common?
Both do hat tricks.

Can August March?
No, but April May.

What's purple and screams?
A damson in distress.

What should you never
forget to take into the
Sahara Desert?
A thirst-aid kit.

What's got four legs, a trunk
and lots of keys?
A piano up a tree.

What did Santa say to his
wife on Christmas Eve?
"Don't go out in
the reindeer."

What do you get if you cross
the Amazonian rainforest
with a map of Norwich?
Very lost.

What kind of water
can't freeze?
Hot water.

What do you get if you stuff
your computer's
disk drive with herbs?
A thyme machine.

Why did the hotel manager ask the talkative chess players to leave his hotel?
He didn't like chess nuts boasting in an open foyer.

Why did the tomato go out with the mushroom?
Because he was a fungi.

How was the Roman Empire cut in half?
With a pair of Caesars.

Where are the Andes?
On the end of the armies.

What's the difference between a photocopier and the measles?
One makes facsimiles and the other makes sick families.

Why was the man with a
photographic memory
so unhappy?
He kept having
negative thoughts.

What did the man
with two left feet
wear to the beach?
Flip-flips.

What's full of holes but
can still hold water?
A sponge.

Where is the best place to
buy computer software?
Washington CD.

What has four wheels and
goes, "Hic! Hic! Hic!"?
A hiccup truck.

What pet is always
found on the floor?
A carpet.

What did the boy say to get
his big brother to give back
his building bricks?
"Lego!"

When is a chair
like a fabric?
When it's sat in.

What should you do if you
need directions in space?
Askeroid.

Did you hear about
the boy who was named
after his father?
He was called "Dad".

What do you call a
man with two left feet?
Whatever you like. If he
tries to catch you, he'll
just run round in circles.

What's the difference
between a crossword expert,
a greedy boy and glue?
One's a good puzzler and
the other's a pud guzzler.
The glue is where
you get stuck.

What's white and yellow
and goes at 125 mph?
A train driver's egg sandwich.

What is ET short for?
So he can touch his toes.

What position in the football
team were the railings?
In defence.

What's brown, hairy
and sneezes?
A coconut with a cold.

What do you do if your
nose goes on strike?
Picket.

What crisps can fly?
Plain crisps.

Did you hear about the
butcher who sat on his
mincing machine?
He got a little behind
in his orders.

What do you call coconut
trees that exercise a lot?
Sweaty palms.

What do snowmen do
in cold weather?
Sit round a candle.

What do snowmen do
in very cold weather?
Light it.

Why did the computer
act crazy?
It had a screw loose.

Where would you find a
rubber trombone?
In an elastic band.

Where was Solomon's
temple?
On his head.

Why did the boy blush when
he opened the fridge?
He saw the salad dressing.

What stays hot
in the fridge?
Chilli sauce.

Which end of a bus is it
best to get off?
It doesn't matter.
Both ends stop.

What did the princess say
while she was waiting for her
photos to arrive?
"Some day my prints
will come!"

Why was the man so
happy that his career
was in ruins?
He was an archaeologist.

What travels around
the world but stays
in a corner?
A stamp.

Why did the cowboy
ride his horse?
Because the horse was
too heavy to carry.

How do footballers
keep cool?
They stand next
to the fans.

Who sits on Cinderella's
keyboard?
Buttons.

What happened when the
plastic surgeon went to
sleep in front of the fire?
He melted.

What do you call an
overweight ET?
An extra cholesterol.

Why do oranges
wear sun block?
Because they peel.

How do you know when
a clock is hungry?
It goes back four seconds.

What happens if you
play table tennis
with a rotten egg?
First it goes ping,
then it goes
pong.

What do you get if you cross
a jogger with an apple pie?
Puff pastry.

What do you get if you
cross a vampire with a
circus entertainer?
Something that goes
straight for the juggler.

When did nerds
rule the Earth?
The Dork Ages.

Why did the sword
swallower go to prison?
He coughed and
injured two people.

What do you call a
dentist in the army?
A drill sergeant.

Why did the golfer wear
two pairs of trousers?
In case he got a
hole in one.

What do you call someone
who makes half-size
models of fish?
A scale modeller.

Why did the robot
need a manicure?
It had rusty nails.

What happened when
the carrot died?
There was a huge
turnip at the funeral.

Why did the man put a
clock under his desk?
He wanted to
work overtime.

What illness do overloaded
Christmas trees get?
Tinselitis.

How does the moon
cut the sun's hair?
Eclipse it.

What has fifty feet
but can't walk?
A tape measure.

Why are rivers so wealthy?
They are lined with banks.

When do computers
go to sleep?
When it's internight.

Where do the police
put trifle thieves?
In custardy.

What did the biscuit say
when he saw his brother
being run over?
"Crumbs!"

What do you call someone
who draws funny pictures
of motor vehicles?
A car-toonist.

Where was the Magna
Carta signed?
At the bottom.

Why did the girl name her
cat "Blacksmith"?
Whenever she called it, it
made a bolt for the door.

What do you get if you
cross a waiter and a
slippery floor?
Flying saucers.

Why shouldn't you believe
a person in bed?
Because he is lying.

Why can't cars
play football?
They've only got one boot.

What's the difference
between bogies
and broccoli?
Children don't eat broccoli.

Why couldn't the parsnip
buy a drink in the pub
one afternoon?
They didn't serve food
after two o'clock.

What can fall thousands of
feet onto iron railings
and not get hurt?
A plane's shadow.

What is a volcano?
A mountain with indigestion.

How do bank robbers
send messages?
By flee mail.

Did you hear about the
man who fell into a
vat of curry?
He slipped into a korma.

What do you call a musical
instrument that is
played by two teams
of twenty people?
A piano forty.

What's short, green
and goes camping?
A boy sprout.

What is the hardest subject?
The study of rocks.

How do you find white shirts
on the Internet?
Use a starch engine.

What do you get if you
cross a pen with
Napoleon's feet?
A footnote in history.

What do you call the owner
of a tool factory?
The vice chairman.

What do you say when an
aeroplane disappears
over the horizon?
Boeing, going, gone.

Where does Tarzan
buy his clothes?
A jungle sale.

What happened when two televisions got married?
It was an awful wedding, but the reception was great.

Who invented King Arthur's round table?
Sir Circumference.

Where were the kings of Albania crowned?
On the head.

Why was Cleopatra so difficult to get on with?
She was the Queen of Denial.

For pigs, what came after the Stone Age and the Bronze Age?
The sausage.

Why was the girl
named Sugar?
Because she was so refined.

What is the cheapest time
to call your friends
long distance?
When they're not home.

What did the orange squash
say to the water?
"I'm diluted to see you!"

Which two words in the
English language have
the most letters?
Post office.

Why are two thieves
like underwear?
Because they're a
pair of nickers.

What tables don't you
have to learn?
Dinner tables.

Who is the oldest singer
on the Internet?
Click Jagger.

What has four wheels
and flies?
A rubbish truck.

What colour is the wind?
Blew.

Why did the tap
dancer leave his job?
He kept falling in the sink.

What are deck chairs
made of?
Beach trees.

How can you prevent
diseases caused by
biting insects?
Don't bite any insects.

What happened to the
girl who wanted a
puppy for Christmas?
She had to have turkey
like everyone else.

Why was the
headmaster worried?
There were too many
rulers in school.

What does Luke Skywalker
shave with?
A laser blade.

What's brown and steaming
and comes out of Cowes?
The Isle of Wight ferry.

Why did the teacher
put the lights on?
The class was so dim.

When does a telephone
work underwater?
When it's wringing wet.

A greengrocer is six feet tall,
has a forty inch waist and
size eleven shoes.
What does he weigh?
Vegetables

What's cold, evil and
lives in a candle?
The wicked wick
of the north.

What do you put in a
www.ashing machine?
Net curtains.

Polar
Escapades

There's an igloo made of ice,
it has ice chairs, ice floors
and ice walls, an ice door
and an ice roof.
What are the stairs made of?
Igloos don't have stairs.

What do you get if you cross
a teddy bear with a pig?
A teddy boar.

What should you call
a bald teddy?
Fred bear.

Where are husky
dogs trained?
In mush rooms.

What animal do you
look like when you
get into the bath?
A little bear.

What steps would you take if an angry polar bear came rushing towards you?
Great big ones.

Why is a polar bear cheap to have as a pet?
It lives on ice.

Why shouldn't you take polar bears to the zoo?
Because they'd rather go to the cinema.

Who ate his animals two by two?
Noah Shark.

What do you get if you cross a giraffe with a husky dog?
An animal that barks at low flying aircraft.

What kind of money do
polar bears use?
Ice lolly.

What's a teddy bear's
favourite pasta?
Tagliateddy.

What do you call a big
white bear with a hole
in his middle?
A polo bear.

Why do polar bears
like bald men?
Because they have a
great, white, bear place.

Have you ever
hunted bear?
No, but I've been
shooting in my shorts.

What is the difference
between Father Christmas
and a warm dog?
Father Christmas wears
a whole suit, a dog just pants.

Why was the little bear
so spoiled?
Because its mother panda'd
to its every whim.

How do you start a
teddy bear race?
Ready, teddy, go.

What do you get if you cross
a snowman and a shark?
Frost bite.

Why don't husky dogs
make good dancers?
They have two left feet.

What do Attila the Hun
and Winnie the Pooh
have in common?
They both have "the" as
their middle names.

What do polar bears
have for lunch?
Ice burgers.

How do you hire
a polar bear?
Put him on stilts.

What do you get if
you cross a polar bear
and a harp?
A bear-faced lyre.

What do you do if your husky
dog eats your pen?
Use a pencil instead.

What's yellow, comes
from Peru and is
completely unknown?
Waterloo Bear, Paddington
Bear's forgotten cousin.

What do you get if you cross
a skunk with a bear?
Winnie the Pooh.

What do you do with
two pieces of bread
in the desert?
Make a sandwich.

What's a husky dog's
favourite hobby?
Collecting fleas.

When does milk
make you blink?
When it is
past-eur-ized.

What did the digital
watch say to his mum?
Look Mum, no hands.

How did the telephones
get married?
In a double ring ceremony.

What do you get if you
cross a US President
with a shark?
Jaws Washington.

Why did the child study
in an aeroplane?

He wanted higher education.

What do you get if you cross
a husky dog and a lion?

A terrified postman.

Why did the boat
go to the dock?

He was sick.

Do you know the time?
No, we haven't met yet.

Why was the broom late?
It over swept.

What kind of hair
do oceans have?
Wavy.

What runs but never walks?
Water.

How do you make
milk shake?
Give it a good scare.

What happened to the
husky dog that ate
nothing but garlic?
Its bark was much
worse than its bite.

What's red and flies and wobbles at the same time?
A jellycopter.

"Waiter, this soup tastes funny."
"Then why aren't you laughing?"

Why did the clock get sick?
It was run down.

Why do you need a licence for a husky dog and not for a cat?
Cats can't drive.

Did you hear about the scientist who invented an acid that could burn through anything?
Now he's trying to invent something to keep it in.

Do you have any
invisible ink?"
"Certainly sir. What colour?"

"Why have you been telling
everyone that I'm an idiot?"
"I'm sorry, I didn't
know it was supposed
to be a secret."

"This match won't light!"
"That's funny, it did
this morning."

What do you call a
husky dog in the middle
of a muddy road?
A mutt in a rut.

"Have you ever seen
a duchess?"
"Yes – it's the same as
an English 's'."

What do you get if you
cross a husky dog
with a blind mole?
A dog that keeps barking
up the wrong tree.

What did the fireman's
wife get for Christmas?
A ladder in her stocking.

What do you get if you
cross a Scottish legend
and a bad egg?
The Loch Ness Pongster.

What has a bottom
at the top?
Your legs.

How do you catch a
runaway husky dog?
Hide behind a tree and
make a noise like a bone.

What is the smelliest
city in America?
Phew York.

"Why are you covered
in bruises?"
"I started to walk through
a revolving door and I
changed my mind."

When is the best time
to buy budgies?
When they're going cheap.

What cheese is made
backwards?
Edam.

What happens when
plumbers die?
They go down the drain.

What kind of meat do you
give a stupid husky dog?
Chump chops.

How do you cure a headache?
Put your head through a
window and the pane
will just disappear.

Why did the sword-swallower
swallow an umbrella?
He wanted to put something
away for a rainy day.

What were the gangster's
last words?
"Who put that violin in
my violin case?"

How many seasons are there
in a husky dog's life?
Just one, the
moulting season.

What do you call an
American drawing?
Yankee doodle.

What do cannibals eat
at tea parties?
Chocolate fingers.

What did one virus
say to another?
"Stay away! I think
I've got penicillin."

What do you call a husky
dog with no legs?
It doesn't matter what you
call him, he still won't come.

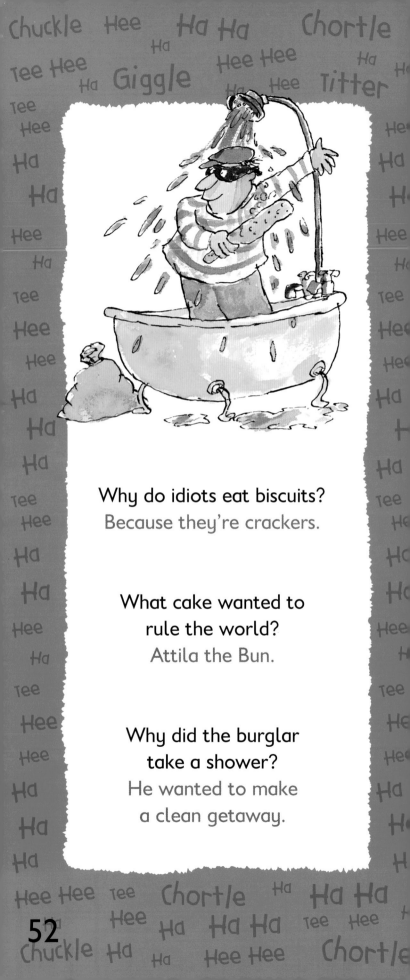

Why do idiots eat biscuits?
Because they're crackers.

What cake wanted to
rule the world?
Attila the Bun.

Why did the burglar
take a shower?
He wanted to make
a clean getaway.

Where does a general
keep his armies?
Up his sleevies.

What's wet, black and jumps
out of the sea shouting
"Knickers!"?
Crude oil.

How did Noah see the
animals in the Ark
at night?
By flood lighting.

What is hairy and coughs?
A coconut with a cold.

What's wet, black and jumps
out of the sea shouting
"Underpants!"?
Refined oil.

What do you call a foreign
body in a chip pan?
An Unidentified
Frying Object.

What did the tie
say to the hat?
You go on ahead and
I'll hang around.

What did the picture
say to the wall?
I've got you covered.

Why was Santa's little
helper depressed?
He had low elf-esteem.

Do you look in the mirror
after you've washed
your face?
No – you usually look
in a towel first.

When is a black dog
not a black dog?
When it's a greyhound.

"Who broke the window?"
"It was Bob, he ducked when
I threw a stone at him."

Why did the lazy man want
a job in a bakery?
So he could loaf around.

"I want a hair cut please."
"Certainly, which one?"

What do you do with
a sick kangaroo?
Give it a hoperation.

Who was the first
underwater spy?
James Pond.

You were a long time putting
salt in the salt-cellar."
"Well, you can't get much
in at a time through those
little holes in the top."

Why did Mickey Mouse
take a trip into space?
He wanted to find Pluto.

Why was the Egyptian
girl worried?
Because her daddy
was a mummy.

What do you get if you cross
two young husky dogs with
a pair of headphones?
Hush puppies.

How old is your grandad?
I don't know but we've
had him a long time.

"Dad, there is a man at the
door collecting for the
new swimming pool."
"Give him a glass of water."

Why is it called a
litter of puppies?
They mess up the
whole house.

"Eat up your spinach, it'll
put colour in your cheeks."
"But I don't want
green cheeks."

What happened when the
wheel was invented?
It caused a revolution.

Did you hear about the mad
scientist who put dynamite
in his fridge?
They say it blew his cool.

What do you call young
husky dogs who have
come in from the snow?
Slush puppies.

"Would you like a duck
egg for tea?"
"Only if you
quack it for me."

Did you hear about
the world's worst
Kamikaze pilot?
He flew forty-two missions.

What city cheats at exams?
Peking.

Why do husky dogs
run in circles?
It's hard to run in squares.

What is the fastest
thing in water?
A motor pike.

Who is in cowboy films
and is always broke?
Skint Eastwood.

Who is the biggest
gangster in the sea?
Al Caprawn.

What do you call a
black husky dog?
A dusky husky.

What do you get if
you cross a husky dog
with a frog?
A dog that can lick
you from the other
side of the road.

Why did the stupid racing
driver make ten pit stops
during the race?
He was asking for directions.

Why is perfume obedient?
Because it is scent
wherever it goes.

When does a husky dog
say "Moo!"?
When it is learning
a new language.

What do you get if you cross
a nun and a chicken?
A pecking order.

What do you call a man
with cow droppings
all over his feet?
An in-cow-poop.

Why didn't the
banana snore?
Because it didn't want
to wake up the rest
of the bunch.

What is a myth?
A female moth.

What do you get if you cross
a husky dog with a skunk?
Rid of the dog.

What's the difference
between electricity
and lightning?
You don't have to
pay for lightning.

What happens to a
husky dog that keeps eating
bits off of the table?
He gets splinters
in his mouth.

What illness did everyone
on the Starship
Enterprise catch?
Chicken Spocks.

What soldiers smell of
salt and pepper?
Seasoned troops.

What is an octopus?
An eight-sided cat.

What did the dog say when
he sat on sandpaper?
"Rufffff."

Can a match box?
No, but a tin can.

What is green and has four
legs and two trunks?
Two seasick tourists.

Why couldn't swamp thing
go to the party?
He was bogged down at work.

Why do mother kangaroos
hate rainy days?
Because the kids have
to play inside.

What kind of dog can jump
higher than a building?
Any dog – buildings
can't jump.

What does a young polar
bear become after it is
four years old?
Five years old.

Why did the dog jump
into the river?
Because he wanted
to catch a catfish.

What is the best year
for a kangaroo?
A leap year.

What does a frog do when
its car breaks down?
Gets it toad off and
jump-started.

What's brown and
sounds like a bell?
Dung.

Why do giraffes have
long necks?
Because they have
smelly feet.

If a dog lost his tail, where would he get another one?
Any re-tail store.

What is a horse's favourite cartoon character?
Whinney the Pooh.

What did the teddy bear say when the monkey offered him dessert?
"No thanks, I'm stuffed."

What do you get if you cross a stream and a brook?
Wet feet.

What do you get if you cross a husky dog with a kangaroo?
A dog that has somewhere to put its own lead.

Which fish can perform
operations?
A sturgeon.

Where are whales weighed?
At a whale-weigh station.

How do you spell mousetrap
in three letters?
"C-A-T".

Where do little fishes
go every morning?
To plaice school.

Where do cats like to
go on holiday?
The Canary Islands.

What would happen if
pigs could fly?
Bacon would go up.

Impish
Incidents

Do zombies eat popcorn
with their fingers?
No, they eat the
fingers separately.

What is a vampire's
favourite sport?
Casketball.

Why does an imp
get indigestion?
Goblin his food.

Why doesn't Dracula
have any friends?
He's a pain in the neck.

Why did the witch feed
her cat with pennies?
She wanted to put some
money in the kitty.

What should you do if
you like Dracula?
Join his fang club.

What do you get if you
cross a vampire
and a pygmy?
A pain in the knee.

What's a vampire's
favourite fast food?
Someone with very high
blood pressure.

How do you join
Dracula's fang club?
Send your name, address
and blood group.

What did the vampire say
when he saw a victim
sleeping peacefully?
"Ahh! Breakfast in bed!"

What did the vampire
say to his victim?
"Your neck's on my list!"

Why was the vampire
heartbroken?
His love was in vein.

What does a ghoul like
most for breakfast?
Rice Creepies.

What do young zombies
call their parents?
Mummy and Deady.

How did the vampire slayer
make holy water?
She took some tap water
and boiled the hell
out of it.

What did Grandpa Ghoul say
to his grandson when he
hadn't seen him for ages?
"You gruesome!"

Why do vampires
drink blood?
Fizzy drinks are bad
for their fangs.

Why do vampires love
school dinners?
They know they
won't get steak.

What is as sharp as a
vampire's fang?
His other fang.

What does a vampire
fear most?
Tooth decay.

Why did Dracula
take up acting?
It was in his blood.

Where did they put Dracula
when he was arrested?
In a blood cell.

What do you give a vampire
with a sore throat?
Coffin medicine.

What groups do
vampires join?
Blood groups.

What does Dracula sing
in the shower?
Fang you for the music.

Why do vampires take
up skateboarding?
They think it's really
ghoul, man.

What do you call a
bloodsucker who
enjoys sleeping in
the great
outdoors?
A campfire
vampire.

What should you do
if a zombie rolls
his eyes at you?
Pick them up and
roll them back.

What TV sitcom do
demons never miss?
Fiends.

What does the baby vampire
say before going to bed?
"Turn on the dark.
I'm afraid of the light."

What are Dracula's
favourite fruits?
Neck-tarines.

Why are zombie football
pitches so wet?
Because the players
dribble all over them.

What's the difference between
a lunatic shouting fish names
and vampires?
One states, "Hake!" and
the others hate stakes.

What is Dracula's
favourite cocktail?
A Bloody Mary.

How do devils protest?
In demon-strations.

What did the mummy
vampire say to her
screaming baby?
"Stop crying, you're
driving me batty."

What's the best way to
get rid of demons?
Plenty of exorcise.

What happened when
two rival vampire sects
started fighting?
Fang warfare.

Why is it so hard to ask
Dracula for a dance?
As soon as he's finished
the fangdango, he goes
into the vaults.

What do elves learn
at school?
The elfabet.

What do vampires love
to have for pudding?
Knickerbocker ghouly.

Where do zombies
stay on holiday?
Anywhere that there's
running rot and mould
in every room.

What's Dracula's
favourite soup?
Scream of tomato.

How did the vampire
cure his sore throat?
By gargoyling.

What do you get if
you cross a vampire
and a mummy?
A gift-wrapped bat.

What do you get if you cross
a werewolf and a vampire?
A fur coat that fangs
around your neck.

How can you tell if you've
been bitten by a vampire?
Every time you have a drink,
your neck leaks.

Why is Dracula such a
successful gymnast?
He loves the vault.

When do vampires bite you?
On wincedays.

What did Godzilla say after
he had eaten London?
"What's for dinner?"

Why are zombies so
tired all the time?
They're dead on their feet.

Why do vampires have
such good marriages?
They're batty about
each other.

What do demons say when
they meet in the morning?
"How the devil are you?"

Did you hear about the
boxer who went looking
for Dracula?
He was out for the count.

Why were the early days
of history called
the dark ages?
There were so
many knights.

Why is everybody bored
of Dracula's artwork?
Because he always
draws blood.

How do you know if a
vampiress likes you?
She bats her eyes.

Where do vampires keep
their savings?
In blood banks.

How do vampires cross
the English Channel?
Blood vessels.

What kind of coffee
do vampires order?
Decoffinated.

Who's the captain of the
graveyard football team?
The ghoulie.

What position did the zombie
play at netball?
Ghoul shooter.

What do zombies
wear in the rain?
Ca-ghouls.

What do vampires say when
they kiss each other?
"Ouch!"

Why can't vampires gamble?
They run away when anyone
puts forward a stake.

How do zombies smell?
Awful.

What happened when the
vampire bit a goose?
He felt down in the mouth.

What do vampire footballers
have at half-time?
Blood oranges.

What do mad axe-men
do at weekends?
Go chopping.

What does Dracula do
when he's angry?
He flips his lid.

What's the difference
between a computer
and a vampire?
One has a byte of memory
and the other has a
memory of bites.

83

Who did the vampire
want to marry?
The girl necks door.

Why did the football
manager sign a horrible,
blood-sucking beast?
Because his team needed
a ghoul to win.

What's worse than
bumping into a vampire?
Bumping into a
thirsty vampire.

Why did the vampire come
top of the class?
Because he passed
his blood test.

Who has the most dangerous
job in Transylvania?
Dracula's dentist.

What did the goblin say
when he came home after
a year abroad?
"Gnome sweet gnome."

What's the first thing a
vampire bites after he gets
his teeth checked?
The dentist.

What did the teacher say
to Dracula after he
failed his maths exam?
"Can't you Count Dracula?"

Why are monsters
covered in wrinkles?
Have you ever tried
to iron a monster?

What do ghouls play
during break time?
Corpse and robbers.

Why don't vampires argue?
Because they'd make
themselves cross.

What type of imp is an
excellent cook?
A hobgoblin.

What kind of vampire
only bites people when
they aren't looking.
A shy one.

Why do vampires have
lentils, chickpeas
and beans with
their meals?
Because they'll eat
anything with pulses.

Why do zombies
love mazes?
All the dead ends.

What comes out after
dark and goes, "Chomp,
suck, ouch!"?
A vampire with a
rotten tooth.

What do you get if you
cross a vampire with a
24-hour clock?
An all-day sucker.

What do you call
a fat vampire?
Draculard.

What do ghouls like
to drink?
Demonade.

Why did Dracula recruit
an apprentice?
He thought he could do
with some new blood.

Why do vampires make
blood-curdling screams?
They're too runny to spread
on their toast otherwise.

What would happen to
a mummy if it fell in
the River Nile?
It would get wet.

Why is Cinderella so
bad at sport?
Because her coach
was a pumpkin.

How many zombies can you
get into an empty grave?
Only one – then it's not
empty any more.

What's woolly, has four legs,
goes baaa and sucks blood?
A lambpire.

What would a mummy do if
it fell in the River Nile?
Climb out again.

What's sweet, red and
doesn't like garlic?
A jampire.

What do you get if you cross
a vampire with a songbird?
Draculark.

What turns into a bat at
midnight and goes oink?
A hampire.

What does Dracula do
when he gets locked
out of his castle?
He goes in through
the bat flap.

Why did the festering
zombie decide to
stay in bed?
He felt rotten.

What do you call
zombie telephones?
Dead ringers.

Where was Dracula
when the lights
suddenly went out?
In the dark.

How does a vampire
clean his house?
With a victim cleaner.

What happens when a
vampire drinks too much?
He gets a fangover.

Why do bats fly at night?
Because they are
afraid to drive.

What is Dracula's
favourite sport?
Bat-minton.

What are the two things that
a vampire can never have
for breakfast?
Lunch and dinner.

What room does a
zombie avoid?
The living room.

What did the zombie say
to his girlfriend?
"What's up, gore-juice?"

What's a vampire's
favourite animal?
A giraffe.

Why was the damsel so tired
after she went
out with Dracula?
It was such a draining
experience.

Why didn't the vampire
need to spend much
money on food?
He eats necks to nothing.

What is a vampire's
favourite pudding?
Adam's apple pie.

Why are vampire
families so close?
Because blood is
thicker than water.

What did the vampire
conductor use?
A bat-on.

What's the difference
between a zombie and a
doughnut?
Have you ever tried
eating a zombie?

Why did the vampire
go to the audition?
He wanted a part he could
get his teeth into.

Why should you avoid a
ghoul's garden party?
It's a fête worse
than death.

Why do vampires brush
their teeth?
To prevent bat breath.

What happened at
the vampire race?
It finished neck and neck.

Why is Hollywood
full of vampires?
They need someone to
play the bit parts.

What did the vampire call his
new false teeth?
A new-fangled device.

What is Dracula's favourite
kind of sausage?
Fangfurters.

Did you hear about the
hopeless vampire slayer?
He used pork chops because
steaks were
too expensive.

What does a zombie have
on his roast beef?
Gravey.

What screams till it
gets what it wants
and flies away?
A spoiled bat.

How many people go
to a zombie's party?
Depends how many
he can dig up.

Why does Dracula wear
patent leather shoes?
Flip-flops don't look good
with a cape and tuxedo.

How can you tell a vampire
is such a fan of cricket?
He turns into a bat
every night.

Why are vampires like
false teeth?

They come out at night.

What kind of pet does
Dracula have?

A bloodhound.

What do you call an
undead cow?

Zombeef.

Where do Chinese
vampires come from?

Fanghai.

Where do zombies
eat lunch?

At the cadaver-teria.

Why did the vampire
explode?

He hit an artery.

Animal Antics

Why won't prawns
share their toys?
They're shellfish.

How does a leopard
change its spots?
Easy, it gets up from
one spot and walks
over to a new one.

What's orange and
sounds like a parrot?
A carrot.

What do you get if you
cross a chicken with an
electricity socket?
A battery hen.

What do you get if you
cross a cow, a sheep
and a baby goat?
The milky baa kid.

What kind of dog loves
to take bubble baths?
A shampoodle.

What do naughty cats leave
behind after a picnic?
Kitty litter.

Why was the monkey taken
in for questioning?
They wanted to gorilla.

What do you get if you cross
a pig with a laundry?
Hogwash.

What goes,
"Clippety–clippety–
clippety"?
A three-legged
horse galloping.

What do toads sit on?
Toadstools.

Which insect makes films?
Steven Spielbug.

If an animal with four legs is
a quadruped and an animal
with two legs is a biped,
what's a zebra?
Stri-ped.

What goes, "Dot-dot-dot-croak, dash-dot-dash-croak…"?
Morse toad.

What insect can be spelled with just one letter?
Bee.

How do you stop a cobra from striking?
Pay it decent wages.

What do you get if you cross a mouse with a bottle of olive oil?
A squeak that oils itself.

What did the parrot say to the spaniel?
"I'm a cocker too."

What did the Pink Panther
say when he stepped
on an ant?
(sing) "Dead ant, dead ant,
dead ant, dead ant, dead ant,
dead ant, dead ant…"

Where do good turkeys
go when they die?
To oven.

What's cool and always
out of breath?
The Pink Panter.

What do you get if you
cross a dog with a
film studio?
Collie-wood.

Why are chickens
so disgusting?
Because they're fowl.

What do you call a chicken
that eats cement?
A bricklayer.

Why was the cow shivering?
It was Friesian.

What fish do you keep
in a birdcage?
A perch.

What do hedgehogs
have for lunch?
Prickled onions.

Why did the zookeeper
split the gnus up?
Because he had good
gnus and bad gnus.

Why did the gorilla log on
to the Internet?
To send chimpanzee-mail.

What do you call a horse
sunbathing behind some
iron railings?
A zebra.

Why didn't the viper
vipe 'er nose?
Because the adder
'ad 'er hanky.

How do Spanish musicians
catch fish?
They castanet.

What is a parrot?
A wordy birdy.

What do you call a parrot
when it has dried itself
after a bath?
Polly unsaturated.

Why did the fly fly?
Because the spider
spied 'er.

What's the difference
between a school dinner
and a pile of slugs?
A school dinner
has a plate.

Why are adolescent
geese so shy?
They get goose pimples.

What do you get if you divide
the circumference of a pig
by its diameter?
Pork pi.

What do you call a bee that
is always complaining?
A grumble bee.

Why are pigs such good
letter writers?
They have loads
of pen pals.

Why do bees have
sticky hair?
Because they have
honeycombs.

What is a bee with
a low buzz?
A mumble bee.

What do you call a juvenile
octopus delinquent?
A crazy, mixed-up squid.

How do you keep flies
out of the kitchen?
Coat the dining room
in manure.

What do two lovesick owls
say when it's raining?
"Too-wet-to-woo!"

What do you get if you
cross a snake with
a building site?
A boa constructor.

What's the difference
between a wolf and a flea?
One howls on the prairie
and the other prowls
on the hairy.

How do you stop moles
digging up your garden?
Hide their spades.

What has four legs, no sense
of humour and flies?
A dead hyena.

What do you call a pig
that studies karate?
A pork chop.

What do you get if
you cross a mountain
with a baby?
A cry for Alp.

What do you call a film
about mallards?
A duckumentary.

Why is it a bad idea to
gamble in the jungle?
There are too many
cheetahs about.

What kind of snake is turned
on when it's raining?
The windscreen viper.

What's the difference
between a fly and a bird?
A bird can fly but
a fly can't bird.

What do you get if you
cross a parrot with
an alarm clock?
Politics.

Why did the woodpecker
with no beak listen to
heavy metal?
It was a headbanger.

What has more lives
than a cat?
A frog it croaks
every night.

What should you do
with a wombat?
Play wom.

What films do
vultures love?
Carrion films

What do you get if
you cross a horse
with a skunk?
Whinny the Pooh.

What's a dog's
favourite city?
New York-ie.

What do you get if you cross
a frog and a rabbit?
Ribbit!

What do you call a rabbit
dressed up as a cake?
A cream bunny.

What did the lobster say
to the rock pool?
"Show me your mussels!"

Why was the butterfly
turned away from
the dance?
Because it was a moth ball.

What do you get if you cross
a bee with a coach?
A buzzzz.

How do lions recharge
their laptops?
They plug them into
the manes.

What's brown and
has a trunk?
A mouse returning
from holiday.

What did the slug
say to the snail?
"Hey, nice crash helmet!"

Why did the two lovesick
deer run away?
They wanted to antelope.

What's cute, brown
and sticky, and eats
eucalyptus leaves?
Coca-koala.

Did you hear about
the skunk that was
shot into space?
It stank to high heaven.

Why did the chicken
cross the web?
To get to the other site.

Where do birds meet
for coffee?
In a nest caf.

Why was the
sheep so itchy?
It was covered in fleece.

When do mice follow cats?
In a dictionary.

Where's Spiderman's
home page?
On the World Wide Web.

Why couldn't the
cow give milk?
It was an udder failure.

Why was the fly-fisherman
so happy?
He caught a four-pound
bluebottle.

What lives in Tibet
and spends too long
on the phone?
A yak.

What do you call an ant
with five pairs of eyes?
Ant-ten-eye.

How many ants does
it take to fill a flat?
Ten ants.

What's the best way to
get a wild hippo?
Find a tame one and
call it names.

What do you call a
blind dinosaur?
I-don't-think-he-saurus.

What do you call a snake
without any clothes on?
Snaked.

What do cats eat
for dessert?
Mice pudding.

What's grey and
squirts you with jam?
A mouse eating
a doughnut.

How does a flea get
from place to place?
By itch-hiking.

Why are snails'
shells so shiny?
They use snail varnish.

What kind of tiles shouldn't
you use for your
bathroom walls?
Reptiles.

What do you get if
you cross a bear
with a freezer?
A teddy brrr.

Why did the bees
go on strike?
For more honey and shorter
working flowers.

Why don't you see millipedes
playing football?
By the time they've laced up
their boots, the final
whistle has blown.

What goes oink,
baaa, moo, quack,
woof, meow?
A multilingual pig.

What book tells you
about chickens?
A hencyclopaedia.

What do you get if
you cross a skeleton
with a dog?
An animal that
buries itself.

What's pink and hard?
A flamingo with a bazooka.

Where do ants buy their
cheese and wine?
Frants.

Why did the man drag a
cabbage on a lead?
He thought it was a collie.

What do you call a camel
with three humps?
Humphrey.

Where do crows
get their beer?
A crowbar.

What do you get if you
cross a cow with a
jogging machine?
A milk shake.

Why do birds fly
south in winter?
It's too far to walk.

What do you get if you cross
a toad with a galaxy?
Star warts.

What lies on the ground
a thousand feet up
and smells?
A dead millipede.

What is the opposite
of restaurant?
Workerant.

Why did the crab
get arrested?
Because he was always
pinching things.

How did the glow worm
feel when someone
stepped on his tail?
De-lighted.

What happens if you
give your mouse some
smelly cheese?
You make an awful mess
of your computer.

How do little rattlesnakes
call home?
Poison-to-poison.

What did the bee say to
its naughty child?
"Please beehive!"

How many skunks does
it take to make a
really big stink?
A phew!

What do you get if you
cross a compass with
a shellfish?
A guided mussel.

Why are owls cleverer
than chickens?
Have you ever
eaten Kentucky
Fried Owl?

Why did the lettuce die?
It got a slug in its heart.

Where do hamsters
come from?
Hamsterdam.

Why did the hedgehog
cross the road?
He wanted to fetch his
squash partner.

What do you get if you
cross a sheep with
a spaceship?
Apollo neck jumper.

How can you get across the
African plains at 60 mph?
Strap yourself to a cheetah.

What do you get if
you cross a penguin
with an elk?
Chocolate moose.

**What did the sow
say to the pig?**
"You take me for grunted."

**How do you catch an
elephant fish?**
Use peanuts for bait.

Why did the lobster blush?
Because the sea weed.

**What's black and white and
never grows up?**
Peter Pan-da.

How do skunks find
their way home?
Instinkt.

What do you call a
rabbit that has its
own private jet?
A millionhare.

What did the banana do
when the monkey chased it?
The banana split.

What do you get if you
cross a kangaroo
with a skyscraper?
A high jumper.

What do you get if you
cross a Shakespeare
play with a pig?
A Ham omelette.

What happened to the prawn
that went to a disco?
It pulled a mussel.

What do you call an
insect that can't
remember the words?
A humbug.

What did the horse say
when it was put in a
field full of thistles?
"Thistle have to do!"

Where do horses spend
their honeymoons?
The bridle suite.

What did the buffalo
say to his son when
he left the house?
"Bison."